Introduction

Being a good sight-reader is so important and it's not difficult at all! If you work through this book carefully – always making sure that you really understand each exercise before you play it, you'll never have problems learning new pieces or doing well at sight-reading in exams!

Using the workbook

1 Rhythmic exercises

Make sure you have grasped these fully before you go on to the melodic exercises: it is vital that you really know how the rhythms work. There are a number of ways to do the exercises – see *Improve your sight-reading* Grade 1 for more details, or these ideas can be downloaded from *fabermusicstore.com* (under the publication title).

2 Melodic exercises

These exercises use the notes (and rhythms) for the Stage, and are organised into Sets which progress gradually. If you want to sight-read fluently and accurately, get into the simple habit of working through each exercise in the following ways before you begin to play it:

- Make sure you understand the rhythm and counting. Clap the exercise through.
- Know what notes you are going to play and the fingering you are going to use.
- Try to hear the piece through in your head. Always play the first note to help.
- Try to experiment with a variety of fingerings in your sight-reading. In some pieces, choosing a more ambitious fingering (which might involve 2nd or 4th position) could produce a better musical result.

3 Prepared pieces

Work your way through the questions first, as these will help you to think about or 'prepare' the piece. Don't begin playing until you are pretty sure you know exactly how the piece goes.

4 Going solo!

It is now up to you to discover the clues in this series of practice pieces. Give yourself about a minute and do your best to understand the piece before you play. Check the rhythms and fingering, hear the piece in your head and then play it confidently.

Always remember to feel the pulse and to keep going steadily once you've begun. Good luck and happy sight-reading!

Terminology:
Bar = measure

Stage 1

Rhythmic exercises

Always count at least two bars before you begin each exercise –
one out loud and one silently.

Melodic exercises

Set 1: Exploring C♯ minor

Grade 6 Violin

Improve your sight-reading!

Paul Harris

Stage 1 **Playing in sharp keys, C♯ minor** *page 4*

Stage 2 **Playing in flat keys, triplets** *page 8*

Stage 3 **$\frac{9}{8}$ and more $\frac{6}{8}$ patterns** *page 12*

Stage 4 **Irregular time signatures, $\frac{5}{4}$ and $\frac{5}{8}$** *page 16*

Stage 5 **Tempo changes, revision** *page 20*

The golden rules *page 24*

Extra Stage: Revision available to download from
fabermusicstore.com

FABER *ff* MUSIC

Practice chart

	Comments (from you, your teacher or parent)	Done!
Stage 1		
Stage 2		
Stage 3		
Stage 4		
Stage 5		

Teacher's name _____

Telephone _____

With many thanks to Gillian Secret for her invaluable help.

© 2011 by Faber Music Ltd
This edition first published in 2011 by Faber Music Ltd.
Bloomsbury House 74–77 Great Russell Street London WC1B 3DA
Music processed by Donald Thomson
Cover and page design by Susan Clarke
Cover illustration by Drew Hillier
Printed in England by Caligraving Ltd
All rights reserved

ISBN10: 0-571-53626-3
EAN13: 978-0-571-53626-9

US edition:
ISBN10: 0-571-53666-2
EAN13: 978-0-571-53666-5

To buy Faber Music publications or to find out about the full range of titles available
please contact your local music retailer or Faber Music sales enquiries:
Faber Music Ltd, Burnt Mill, Elizabeth Way, Harlow CM20 2HX
Tel: +44 (0) 1279 82 89 82   Fax: +44 (0) 1279 82 89 83
sales@fabermusic.com   fabermusicstore.com

Listen
Think (why does it sound off)
Fix what sounds off
go slow

Violin

The Violinist's Wedding Album
for Violin and Keyboard

1. Canon

Johann Pachelbel; arr. Latham

EDELWEISS
(From "THE SOUND OF MUSIC")

Lyrics by OSCAR HAMMERSTEIN II
Music by RICHARD RODGERS

Violin

Violin

2. Trumpet Tune

Henry Purcell; arr. Latham

Allegro maestoso

Twenty Études in the Second, Third, Fourth and Fifth Positions.

Hans Sitt. Op. 32, Book II.

2te Lage.

2d Position.

21. Allegro.

2te Lage.　　　　　　　　　2d Position.

Moderato.

25.

5<u>te</u> Lage. 5th Position.

Moderato.

37.

Set 2: Exploring other sharp keys

Prepared pieces

1 Play the scale and arpeggio in a variety of dynamics from the piece and then in the style of the piece.

2 Choose a suitable rhythmic pattern (of about two bars) and hear it in your head. Now improvise a short piece on the rhythm.

3 Think through how you will finger the piece. Then think through the bowing.

4 Tap the pulse and think the rhythm, then tap the rhythm and think the pulse.

5 Give a performance in your head, then play the piece with great confidence.

Spaghetti tarantella

Stand up

Going solo! Don't forget to prepare each piece carefully before you play it.

Look before you leap

In a hurry

With a hint of JSB

Stage 2

Rhythmic exercises

Make sure all three notes in a triplet are the same length.

Melodic exercises

Set 1: Exploring triplets in major keys

Set 2: Exploring triplets in minor keys

Set 3: Exploring more flat keys

Prepared pieces

1 Play the scale and arpeggio in the character of the piece.

2 Walk around the room in time, and think or sing the rhythm.

3 Think through the bowing of the piece, in particular the bow speed.

4 Make up an exercise or short piece which continually alternates ♩♪ and ♪♪♪

5 Play the first note and hear the piece through in your head, with musical expression.

Enjoy your triplet!

Three for the price of two

Going solo! Don't forget to prepare each piece carefully before you play it.

Waiting for a bus

Don't triplet over

Stage 3

Rhythmic exercises

1

2

3

Melodic exercises

Set 1: Exploring 9/8 time

1 — Allegretto — *mf*

2 — Andante — *p*

3 — Allegro — *mp*

4 — Con brio — *f*

Set 2: Exploring more rhythms in $\frac{6}{8}$ and $\frac{9}{8}$

Prepared pieces

1 Play the scale and arpeggio in a lively manner, with energy and colour, using dynamics from the piece.

2 Set a pulse going and hear the piece through in your head *at the same time.*

3 Think through the fingering and the bowing.

4 Improvise in the key in $\frac{6}{8}$ or $\frac{9}{8}$ time. Make your improvisation quite long so you can immerse yourself in the music.

5 Play the first note and hear the piece through in your head, including musical expression.

Busy texting

Magic spell

Going solo! Don't forget to prepare each piece carefully before you play it.

Ballet of the Bohemian bow-makers

Ballet of the scrolls and chin-rests

Stage 4

Rhythmic exercises

Irregular time signatures are no more difficult than regular ones. Simply keep a strong feel for the beat: ♩ in $\frac{5}{4}$ and ♪ in $\frac{5}{8}$. Bars will be divided into 3+2 or 2+3 groupings, which usually become apparent from the pattern of notes.

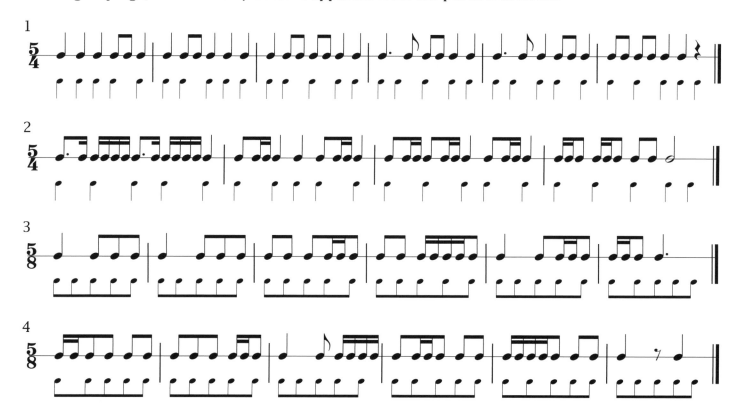

Melodic exercises

Set 1 : Exploring $\frac{5}{4}$

Look through each piece and decide whether it is in 3+2 or 2+3 groupings.

Set 2: Exploring $\frac{5}{8}$

Prepared pieces

1 Play the scale in groups of 5.

2 Is the piece in groups of 3+2 or 2+3? How will this affect your performance?

3 Think about bowing and the fingering.

4 Tap the pulse with one hand and the rhythm with the other.

5 Play the first note and think through the performance, complete with character and dynamics.

Song and dance

Trying to ride a bicycle up a hill on a wet Wednesday evening

Going solo! Don't forget to prepare each piece carefully before you play it.

Stage 5

Rhythmic exercises

Melodic exercises

Prepared pieces

1 Play the scale using as many of the marked dynamics as you can. Then play it staccato.

2 Think about the B♯s and A♯s.

3 Think through the fingering.

4 Tap the pulse strongly and think the rhythm, then tap the rhythm softly and think the pulse.

5 Imagine playing the piece through confidently.

A jolly jaunt in July

Your dial-a-pizza has arrived!

Going solo! Don't forget to prepare each piece carefully before you play it.

Mozart has a nap

A rhinoceros and a sloth have a conversation

The golden rules

A sight-reading checklist

Before you begin to play a piece at sight, always consider the following:

1 Look at the piece for about half a minute and try to feel that you are *understanding* what you see (just like reading these words).

2 Look at the time signature and decide how you will count the piece.

3 Look at the key signature and think about how to finger the notes.

4 Notice patterns – especially those that repeat, or are based on scales and arpeggios.

5 Notice any markings that will help you convey the character.

6 Don't begin until you think you are going to play the piece accurately.

7 Count at least one bar in.

When performing a sight-reading piece

1 Keep feeling the pulse.

2 Keep going at a steady tempo.

3 Remember the finger pattern of the key you are in.

4 Ignore mistakes.

5 Look ahead – at least to the next note.

6 Play musically, always trying to convey the character of the music.